Poems and Photographs by
Linda Joy Montgomery

Copyright   2001   Linda Joy Montgomery
                   Initial Edition 1989
                   Second Printing 1993
                   Expanded Edition 2001

Published by   Divine Designs
                    P.O. Box 162
                    Black Mountain, NC 28711

Printed in China by   Oceanic Graphic Printing, Englewood Cliffs, NJ
Graphic Design by   Hannah Kleber, Kleber Graphic Design
                       Expanded Edition: Cynthia Frederick, Precision Graphics

ISBN 0-9624768-1-1
Library of Congress Catalog Card Number: 89-81213

Silent Strength

Sometimes I get lost in the world.
Caught in confusion, afraid of being alone.
I may have lost my way.
In panic it feels like darkness;
I struggle to find the Light.

If I can remember
Time and time again
To stop, to pause, to know,
To reach inside myself,
God's loving presence is there.

It is so subtle,
Like a gentle wind.
I must become still
In the midst of this raging storm,
In order to feel
The tender touch of God's love.

Like the newness of the sweet early dawn,
Wrapped in softness, it comes.
This warm feeling expands,
Freeing my heart from fear.
I allow this cozy warmth to overtake me,
Giving way,
Like melting under the covers of a comforter
On a cold, crisp afternoon.

The feeling is so delicious
That I wonder how I ever
Could have been afraid.

My mind toys
With the illusion of fear,
Tantalizing it, taunting it,
Until it becomes somehow real.
I must now succumb to these fascinations
That penetrate the world's reality.

My reality is God.
I am enfolded
In the loving arms of the Divine.
This presence lives inside me.
It is the fabric of my being.
It is the sound of peace.
I can hear it if I am
Very, very still.

A sound that goes beyond all sounds,
And yet it resonates, like a song within me.
When I feel this peace there is no time,
Only the perfection of God's grace,
And life smiling at me.

Behold Beauty

What is beauty when you can't see it with your eyes?
I long to see the array of autumn colors in the trees.
I want to witness the first parade of
    daffodils in the spring.
I want to cast my gaze over the sea and
    the expanse of the sky,
Allowing my sight to be captured by the
    movement of a bird in flight,
Or a boat bobbing in the waves.

    I remember the sand aglow with the golden light of dawn
    Shimmering as the ocean draws the water back into itself.
    I remember the stillness of night in the mountains
    When the heavens would boast bright, beautiful stars,
    The thrill of it would make me tingle with awe.

        Where is this beauty I long to see?
        I know it is there in sparkling gems.
        It twinkles in the eyes of friends and lovers,
        And paints a smile on children's faces.
        When I feel this longing to see
        I know I am so very close.
        In this moment,
        I long to embrace and I long to withdraw.

My spirit will not let me forget
That all these images are a part of me.
God offers me gifts, symbols of beauty and Light,
Currents of thoughts and visions that
    sometimes bring me to tears.
The tears are not those of hurt of sadness,
But a letting go of the past.

This is not an easy place to come to.
The road is full of pitfalls—
Of fear, anxiety, and crowded memories.
Yet, as those emotions clear,
Like the sun breaking through the clouds,
I behold beauty.

It is the beauty of my soul
Expanding to the music of God's presence.
It is a beauty that allows me to feel
    the flutter of angels,
The peace of twilight,
And the delight of a new day.
I am the beauty of God's Love.
I am that Light, a shining essence.
I am a flower,
A jewel...
A rainbow...
I am God's beauty.

Daybreak

Light mingles with the sky
The glow of sunrise begins,
A great ball of sun yawns
And stretches its rays into the world.
As it awakens, birds sing,
Insects clamor in delight.
This golden glow shines into creation,
Loving everything.

The sun ignites a spark in me.
I want to dance, to sing, to play,
To shine.

The sun is a happy being.
I think he laughs a lot.
He likes to chuckle.
He muses at me when I fret and frown,
"Life is cheerful and happy,
    look to me," says the sun.
"Be the light as I am,
    share your Love with the World,
And shine brightly for all to see.
Be radiant. Be alive."

Reflections

When time is no longer itself
It offers graciously to give way
    to a flood of warmth and love.
The moment is full, and yet empty.
My heart is brimming with a soft radiance.
Sometimes alone, sometimes with another,
And often in the rapture of nature
Grace comes.

The air is hushed and the light casts no shadows.
It shines gloriously in that moment
Into every particle of being and thought.
Radiant in its essence, it permeates the stillness,
Bringing to it a special embrace.
There is no going and no coming.
There is no thought of staying or leaving,
Only Being, merging with the softness
    of surrounding warmth.

What else could be so encompassing?
Being warmed by showering rays of sunlight?
Embraced by the caring arms of another?
These flood the senses with delight and yet
Grace resonates more deeply,
Filling the soul with a passion for life.
This love goes beyond a single focus,
Touching everything with a magical presence,
Embracing all her wonder.

Grace comes in the silence of knowing,
In the stillness of truth,
In the awareness
That God's presence is in all things.

Two Hearts

Two hearts waiting for the wind;
The winds of time, the winds of love,
The winds of heaven.
Sailing on the lake of life
Calm, serene and still.
Going nowhere and yet going everywhere.

One heart awaits the ripple of the wind
To catch the fancy of the sail,
To quicken the journey—
Anxious for sensation of movement.

Isn't life a dance of movement?
A rush of feeling?

The other heart watches,
Content with contemplation, ease and patience.
Here, now, in this place
There is no reason to race.
The mind is full with the beauty of
The shoreline, the sky, the trees,
The sunlight fixing its gaze upon the water.

For the other a gentle breeze is welcome.
Soft waves of desire lap against the boat
And tug at consciousness.
Is there more, something more?

This love that springs forth eternal
Must have a source; it must have a name—
It must be in the winds of change,
Of growth, of Spirit.

"Take my hand," one heart calls out to the other.
"And we shall run free on the sands of time, feeling
The sun in our faces and the wind at our backs.

And we shall play in the waves of the sea
And dive and swim and laugh and sing
Until we are full of this love of life."

The other heart smiles, "And what of this precious moment?
Are we not full of the sun's rays?
Isn't our love as full and
Beautiful as a bouquet of flowers, ever blossoming
Into new dimensions of awareness?

Are we not each rainbows, radiating colors and
Virtues of hope and beauty and wonder in the stillness of
Our existence?"

In this magical moment we meet.

Two hearts waiting for the wind.
One stops to pause, the other looks up.
There is one heart, one life, one essence.

Life is a Kaleidoscope

Changing patterns, changing concepts, changing colors,
The kaleidoscope of my being is shifting.

New life is emerging,
Like a growing seed pushing up through the soil.
There is struggle, change, transformation.
I am called to let go of the past.
I am drawn into the newness of this moment,
To see the beauty of each kaleidoscopic pattern,
To acknowledge the gift of each experience,
And to let them go.

Bits of colored glass are rearranging themselves
And I glimpse the perfection of symmetry.
I cannot preserve the pattern.
However carefully I put down the kaleidoscope,
The pattern changes.
What is it that makes me want time to stand still?
I fear that the gold I hold in my hand will turn to sand,
That the road I am following will find its end.

I am reminded of God's loving presence.
If I live in the consciousness of Love,
Each moment can be more beautiful than the last.
Life then becomes a collection of precious gems,
Not bits and pieces of colored glass.
I feel the deep blue peace of sapphires,
The passion of rubies,
The healing green of emeralds.

Sometimes I search for treasure, and yet,
If I am calm and poised,
The gift in each moment is revealed.
I am called to acknowledge these gifts.
Each lesson, each experience, allows me to become
Something greater.

When I'm most lost and confused,
It's helpful to remember—
My Life is a kaleidoscope
Of ever changing thoughts and patterns,
Evolving into a multi-faceted perspective.
Joy, Truth, Harmony and Balance,
Are rearranging themselves
So I can stretch and expand and reach for the Light.

Remembrance

This is not a dream
That floats on the breath of slumber,
Weaving fantasy in the night.
Nor is it a playful fascination
That skips through my mind
Like thoughts of a summer day.

I hear a whisper in the wind
And I feel its soft caress.
There is a remembrance
Of caring and sharing
Beyond this place, beyond this time.

I honored this presence once
With a symbol of enduring love.
A rose, offered and accepted
In a moment that sidestepped syncopated time.

It was as if we danced to a song
While the music played somewhere else.
This tune flirted with the clink of glasses
And dodged our conversation—
Much like a game of hide-and-seek.

Special moments in the past call forth
A rush of feelings in the present.
What are these feelings
That have little tie to time?
They surface in the moment
When time is still.

I cannot reach for the future,
Nor can I seize the past,
So I open to the present — to Love.
The rosy warmth is welcome,
And I know beyond all else
My soul remembers.

Wisdom

What is this sense
That fills the spaces between my thoughts?
It is a substance
That floats delicately in clear Light.

    Wisdom—it has its own power and strength
    Like the silence of growing trees.
    Reaching up toward the heavens,
    They fill the air with the presence of majesty.

        Yet wisdom cannot be drawn
        By the stroke of the imagination.
        Its texture cannot be touched or sculpted into form.
        It is an ethereal essence
        Which can only be approached by images.

            To know wisdom
            Is to lose one's self in its presence.
            The outline of identity fades gloriously
            Into a mixture of color and Light.

In that moment
There is no beginning and no end.
All life becomes connected
In the oneness of Being.

Wisdom is permeable and soft,
Yet its substance is radiant and full.
It is an embrace of perfection,
A dance of joy,
A fountain of Light.

In this moment of newness
There is discovery without fear.
There is a knowing embrace of love,
A feeling of warmth and protection.

Wisdom rests in clarity.
It floats in the space between thoughts and emotions,
Where there is neither rush of wind
Nor scurry of time.

Rooted to the Earth

Seeds of awareness are planted
In the soil of my soul,
Awaiting the nourishment
Of love and recognition.
Reaching skyward, the blossom bursts open,
Embracing the spheres of heaven.

The flower is bright and beautiful.
It captivates me.
It draws me into myself,
As I feel the flowering of my soul.

I have come to enjoy
Reaching for the Light.
I have focused intently
On the wonders of Divine ecstasy.
How is it that I have not remembered
That this plant also has roots?

As this flower shoots upward,
The roots of awareness penetrate
Deeply into the earth.
My soul is as much a part
Of earth awareness
As it is the songs of heaven.

I am connected to this planet.
I must allow
This root system to grow,
So that I can draw
Healing strength from the earth.
The earth beckons me.
It reminds me that I am a part of it
And it is a part of me.

I love to soar higher and higher,
Buoyed by air, and Light, and angels.
Now I can see
That I must expand my awareness
To include the ground I walk on.
I allow my roots to extend
To embrace this loving planet.

I have favored rainbows and stars and sunlight.
Now it is time—time to know
That I have been planted here
To bring my awareness
Into a balance of heaven and earth.

Royal Splendor

There was a time, in heightened awareness,
I saw a flower blossoming in my heart.
It was the most beautiful flower
I had ever seen, lavender laced with gold.

I wanted to pick this flower
And offer it to you,
In all of its royal splendor.
I wanted to give you beauty and love.

But this flower in my heart
Was not to be given.
I had always seen love as something to be shared,
A life created together, a synthesis of being.
Now this symphony of color and harmony
Was playing in my heart.
This Love, this flower existed
Only for me.

I decided then, if I could grow
A bushel of flowers,
I would gather for you
    a most beautiful bouquet.

But I have learned to pause,
    to look, to understand,
To seek the divine wisdom
That comes to me in symbols of beauty.
Often, I am given a symbol
Of God's love for me—
    a gift of hope,
A present of strength, a treasure of truth.
As I nurture the flowers of beauty in my heart,
They become more and more living symbols
Of this deepening Love.

Although I'd love to pick you a bouquet,
    I think not.
Instead, I would invite you
To walk with me
    in the garden of my heart,
To praise the glory of God,
And to share the wonderful symbols
that have helped me grow.

Come Play with Me

I invite the newness of this moment
Into my heart.
The rush of the wind,
The falling of rain drops,
The bursting of sunlight.
I embrace this energy of life.

Come play with me.
Let us dance in the glory of God's love
And sing a song of joy to the world.
Happiness floats on the wind
Waiting to be breathed and celebrated.

Oh spirit of life that makes gardens grow and birds sing,
Come play with me and let my soul take flight.
Like sunlight we will create dancing stars on the water.
We will laugh with the leaves and turn our backs to the wind.
We will become crystals and wrap rainbows around all people,
Filling their hearts with joy.

Come play with me.
We shall water the flowers of souls
And delight in the beauty of their blossoms.
It is my choice to live in paradise,
To play, to laugh, to love,
To celebrate life,
To embrace each moment with the fullness of my heart.

The Song of Earth

As I place my bare feet on the grass,
I am filled with the Song of the Earth.
Her sweet melody rushes into me
And I feel my soul overflow with Joy.

My heart expands to embrace this loved one;
It feels like coming home.
As I relax into this enveloping warmth,
I feel Her soft presence around me.

I can easily imagine myself
Dancing through trees and
    wading through meadows,
Admiring precious flowers
And contemplating the peace
    of a flowing stream.

The Song of Earth—
    how deep and sweet this resonance.
Gently, She pulls me into herself,
Washing away my tears,
Mending my sorrows.

In this Oneness, there is only Love,
Compassion for Being, and Divine Radiance.
In this Presence, all my fears give way
To a new, bubbling spring of Joy.

Listening

Softly—a voice speaks:

Honor yourself.
Praise the light that burns brightly within,
And know that you are a blessing.
Drink from the golden chalice
And allow the sweet nectar of Divine Love
      to fill you.
This golden liquid is esconced with Light.

Love yourself.
Give way to a flood of feeling
That bubbles up from inside.
Follow it to its source—
The path lies before you.
Energy, Light, Love, Joy
Expressing, seeking, giving—
Now it is time—time to feel
The unique expression that you are.

Allow yourself to bask
In the sunlight of your soul.
Know that you are specia,l
A blend of talents and grace,
      frivolity and love,
            humor and expectancy.
Honor this gift that you are.

      Let your attention drop away from appearances
      To focus on the Divine expression
      Of your total Being.
      Feel your connectedness
      With Life and with Love.

            Journey each day into this special place
            Of calmness and knowing.
            Feel the magnitude of the great love
            Of your indwelling spirit
            Allow all parts of yourself to merge
            In this glowing energy.
            Experience the peace of your being.
            Go beyond thoughts.
            Allow feelings to dissolve.
            Let go of all tension,
            And rest before the altar of your heart.

A Pelican's Dream

Fly free
In the salt air that floats above the ocean.
Free to explore
The expanse of blue that surrounds you.
There are no limits,
Only freedom for your heart to soar
Higher and higher with the wind.

Dance in the sun
And feel the joy
Of wings outstretched.
Gracefully you skim
Over the waters of earth awareness,
Amused yet sometimes challenged
By the shadow of thoughts and emotions.

The air rushing through you
Strengthens you.

You are the one with the Divine essence.
The energy of the air keeps your heart open,
Your mind clear, your body strong,
And love ever-present.

The ocean is full of colorful fantasies
Ready to be seized in the moment
When the water is clear and time stands still.
A rush of knowing tells you when the time is right
And the gift is yours.

What a joy to embrace this energy of the moment,
To dive deep into the clear blue sea.
You emerge triumphant,
Glowing with the thrill of God's creation.

You are free
To feel the sun, the air, the water,
To play with light and shadow,
To follow your dreams,
To fly.

Joy—Presents or Presence?

I remember as a child
    being wide-eyed with wonder
Running down the stairs on Christmas morning
    to find a special present just for me.

I was surrounded by packages dressed
    in bright shiny ribbons
    full of color and mystery,
Each a carefully wrapped bundle of love.
The sheer delight of it made me light up
    like the Christmas tree itself.
And I could feel my heart glowing on the inside.

Presents—they are magical.
They tell us we are loved,
That we are special.
They bring us joy,
    the joy of giving and the
    joy of receiving.
Looking back, why did I feel saddened
At the passing of Christmas?
We seem to put away our joy
    with the boxes and bits of ribbon,
Thinking this special feeling
    will come again next year.

The fascination of colors and tinsel
    excites us,
It triggers an expectancy
    of an outpouring of love.
Could it be that love and joy are
    stored in our hearts,
Which we open like packages
    on special occasions?

Joy is not contained in the heart
    or in a package wrapped with
    a bright red ribbon.
It is our feeling for life,
    our reverence for being
    and for loving.
It is the special knowing
    that we are always embraced
By God's presence.
The shiny presents under the tree
    are symbols of
God's abiding love,
    presented to us in every moment.

In the silence of being,
   in the beauty of nature,
   in the heartfelt exchange
   of giving and receiving,
   joy is there.
It knows no limits
It is the Divine Presence.
Subtle yet powerful,
Momentary, yet timeless.

This loving warmth
   floods every cell and
   every thought.
Invite this presence
   into your life.
Allow the joy of living, loving
   and being loved
   to hold you.
Living the joy of Christmas
   every day
Is the awareness
   of Divine Love.

Change

Change can be challenging:
It pulls us from our comfort zones,
Enticing us to draw on measures of
Security that seem to have fueled our existence.

In the flux of time and expectations
We feel fragmented by our agendas and
Frustrated with our projections.
The past has become distant, the future unknown.

How do we get back on track?
Perhaps there is no prescribed course.
Our existence is now being carved by
The creativity that comes forth in every moment.
We are guided by inner promptings,
Centered in peace and divine wisdom.

We must go beyond our reliance
On our own actions and those of others,
Thinking they will yield desired results.
We can now open to a deeper
Trust that Spirit is guiding us to be
In the right place at the right time,
For reasons we may not fully comprehend.

Every day holds new promise,
A new use for our energies.
Can we remain open to the mystery-
Knowing, that all is in perfect alignment?

With a strong sense of trust,
The right things will come about.
Events will unfold in perfect sequence,
Often beyond the schemes of our mind.

Indeed, change is disconcerting.
Yet, it offers opportunities to expand
Our outlook and to gain new perspective.

Embrace the newness of each day,
Innocent like a child,
Open to what might unfold,
With a sense of adventure and delight.

Grief and Grace

A torrent of tears gushes forth,
Rising from an underground river,
Buried from my awareness.

Waves of sadness wash over me,
At the passing of a loved one.
The pain of loss
Brings feelings that surge forth,
Lashing out and objecting
To the bounds of limitation.

My mind wants to thwart the
Passage of time-to open it,
To free it from the shackles
I've placed upon it.

In my life, I can see now
That my desire to rush,
To always do more, stems
From a place of discontent, a
Feeling of a lack of wholeness.

Interesting, how those people around us
Become mirrors for our awareness.
They might well appreciate our gifts-
And yet, their love and clarity
Provide a reflecting pool to see that
Which we have hidden from ourselves.

Waves of emotion stir
The sandy bottom underneath,
Rustling the shells and settled particles
In a churning tumultuous current.

These waves offer the promise
Of movement, change, and growth-
As, one by one, they
Draw back into the great
Sea of spiritual awareness.

Beyond

For Randy

My eyes could see once
The lovely early morning light,
Simple things–like blades of grass, buds of flowers,
A multitude of expressions on people's faces.

I read the world with my eyes,
Moving through light and shadow,
Often seduced by form,
Captivated by appearances.

Now, I no longer see
The look on people's faces.
Rather, I know them by their tone
And by their openness.

Sounds and smells of nature
Are more vivid,
And I can sense with keenness
The loving energy of Earth.

Awareness is wonderfully heightened
By this new warmth of feeling.
I can see more fully through the Love in my heart.

I know you used your legs once,
Moving through the world as I did
With a sense of freedom and independence.
I know you remember walking and running,
And taking sides for dodge ball.

Now, without the use of your legs,
It is a new perspective–
Feeling, searching, knowing–
The limits of this body structure.

Perhaps in this time of seeming limitation,
You, too, are directed
To open your heart.

Your heart is the gateway to Spirit.
Spirit is soaring freedom, beyond body experience.
You are free to explore
The vast sensations of Being;
Diving into Oneness merging with Love,
Floating in bliss, resonating in attunement.

Stand tall in the knowledge of who you are.
Stand in the center of your heart.
Live from this place, surrounded by the knowing of your Spirit.

From our hearts, you and I can see, and we can stand.
We can see the souls of others,
And respond to their Light.
We can stand on our true knowing
And project it out to the world.

The Source

There is a deep river that flows
Through the canyons of my being.
Having looked everywhere,
I return
To the source, deep within myself.

    For sometime, I have been content
    To frequent the rim of the canyon.
    Admiring the depths of my being,
    I've watched the play of Light
    On the striations of my experiences,
    The layers of my life.

        Seeing the many colors and patterns,
        I marvel at God's handiwork–
        The illumination of lessons,
        The acceleration of growth,
        The manifestation of miracles.

           These fascinations with phenomena and the past
           Have now given way to a deeper quest–
           A quest for the Source of truth.

I must not be afraid of falling,
As I descend the narrow rocky trail
To the floor of the canyon.
When I reach that peaceful place
I will find the river.

The river is energy,
The river is Love, flowing continuously.
There is no beginning, there is no end–
Only pure Divine substance.
It invites me into itself.

I allow myself to be washed and cleansed,
To be made new by this Holy water.
And so I come away relaxed, refreshed,
Knowing that God invites me to experience the Source,
The deep river in the canyons of my being.

Meadows To Go?

I'd like some lovely, luscious meadows
Bathed in creamy golden light—
Wrapped in softness and early morning dew.
Fill them with wonder,
These fields of grace
That echo a song in the wind.
Sprinkle them with wildflowers
Like Colorado in July
And add just the lightest touch of magic.

As if this is not enough,
I'd like a lofty rise of mountain peaks,
Dusted with bright, white snow.
Place all of this in a large shimmering bubble
And tie it gently with rainbows.